EMMANUEL JOSEPH

The Connected Table, How Food, Robots, and Society Bring Us Together

Copyright © 2025 by Emmanuel Joseph

All rights reserved. No part of this publication may be reproduced, stored or transmitted in any form or by any means, electronic, mechanical, photocopying, recording, scanning, or otherwise without written permission from the publisher. It is illegal to copy this book, post it to a website, or distribute it by any other means without permission.

First edition

This book was professionally typeset on Reedsy.
Find out more at reedsy.com

Contents

1. Chapter 1: The Universal Language of Food — 1
2. Chapter 2: The Evolution of Dining: From Hearth to High-Tech — 3
3. Chapter 3: Robots in the Kitchen: The New Frontier — 5
4. Chapter 4: The Social Impact of Automated Dining — 7
5. Chapter 5: The Intersection of Tradition and Innovation — 9
6. Chapter 6: Dining in the Digital Age — 11
7. Chapter 7: The Role of Technology in Sustainable Food... — 13
8. Chapter 8: The Future of Dining: Trends and Innovations — 15
9. Chapter 9: The Impact of Globalization on Food Culture — 17
10. Chapter 10: Food and Community: Building Connections Through... — 19
11. Chapter 11: The Ethics of Eating: Navigating Food Choices — 21
12. Chapter 12: A Vision for the Future: Food, Robots, and... — 23
13. Chapter 13: The Emotional Connection: Food and Memory — 25
14. Chapter 14: The Science of Flavor: Understanding Taste and... — 27
15. Chapter 15: Food and Health: Nourishing Body and Mind — 29
16. Chapter 16: Culinary Creativity: The Art of Innovation in... — 31
17. Chapter 17: Food as Cultural Diplomacy: Bridging Divides — 33

1

Chapter 1: The Universal Language of Food

Food has always played a crucial role in human culture, transcending boundaries of geography, ethnicity, and language. It is a universal language that brings people together, fostering connections and creating shared experiences. In every corner of the world, food traditions reflect the history, values, and aspirations of communities. From family dinners to festive celebrations, food acts as a medium through which we express love, hospitality, and belonging.

The simple act of sharing a meal can bridge cultural divides and promote understanding among diverse groups. When we sit down to eat, we engage in a communal ritual that reinforces social bonds and creates a sense of unity. Food has the power to evoke memories, transport us to different times and places, and connect us with our heritage. It is through food that we learn about each other's customs, beliefs, and ways of life.

In today's globalized world, food continues to play a vital role in fostering intercultural dialogue. With the advent of technology and social media, culinary traditions are more accessible than ever before. People can explore diverse cuisines, experiment with new recipes, and share their culinary creations with others around the globe. This exchange of culinary knowledge and practices enriches our lives and deepens our appreciation for the world's cultural diversity.

As we move forward, it is essential to recognize the importance of preserving and celebrating food traditions. By doing so, we honor our ancestors, promote cultural heritage, and ensure that future generations can experience the joy and connection that comes from sharing a meal. The universal language of food has the potential to unite us in our shared humanity and create a more inclusive and compassionate world.

2

Chapter 2: The Evolution of Dining: From Hearth to High-Tech

The history of dining is a testament to human ingenuity and adaptability. From the humble hearths of ancient civilizations to the high-tech kitchens of today, our approach to preparing and consuming food has evolved dramatically. In the early days, cooking was a communal activity centered around a fire, where families and communities gathered to share sustenance and stories. The hearth was not only a source of warmth and nourishment but also a focal point of social interaction.

As societies advanced, so did their culinary techniques and tools. The development of agriculture, trade, and urbanization brought new ingredients, flavors, and cooking methods into the fold. Kitchens became more specialized and efficient, with innovations like the stove, oven, and refrigerator transforming the way we cook and store food. The dining experience itself also evolved, with the advent of formal dining rooms, restaurants, and cafes providing new venues for social engagement.

In the modern era, technology has revolutionized the way we approach food and dining. From smart appliances and automated cooking devices to online recipe databases and food delivery services, the possibilities are endless. These advancements have made cooking more accessible, efficient, and enjoyable, allowing people to experiment with new cuisines and techniques from the comfort of their own homes. The integration of robotics and artificial intelligence in the kitchen is poised to take this evolution even further, with innovations like robotic chefs and automated meal planning systems becoming increasingly common.

As we embrace these technological advancements, it is essential to balance convenience with tradition. While modern tools can enhance our culinary capabilities, they should not replace the human touch and creativity that make cooking a deeply personal and meaningful activity. By preserving the rich history and cultural significance of dining, we can ensure that the evolution of food continues to enrich our lives and bring us together.

3

Chapter 3: Robots in the Kitchen: The New Frontier

The integration of robots and automation in the kitchen represents the latest frontier in culinary innovation. From robotic chefs to automated food preparation systems, these technological advancements have the potential to revolutionize the way we cook and dine. One of the most significant benefits of robots in the kitchen is their ability to perform repetitive and labor-intensive tasks with precision and efficiency, freeing up human chefs to focus on creativity and experimentation.

Robotic chefs, equipped with advanced sensors and machine learning algorithms, can replicate complex culinary techniques and produce consistent, high-quality dishes. These robots can chop, stir, sauté, and even plate food with remarkable accuracy, ensuring that every meal is prepared to perfection. In addition to enhancing the efficiency of food preparation, robots can also help reduce food waste by optimizing portion sizes and minimizing human error.

The use of robots in the kitchen is not limited to professional settings; home cooks can also benefit from these innovations. Smart kitchen appliances, such as robotic cooking assistants and automated meal planning systems, make it easier for individuals to prepare healthy and delicious meals at home. These devices can suggest recipes based on available ingredients, provide step-by-step cooking instructions, and even adjust cooking times and temperatures to ensure optimal results. As a result, people can enjoy the benefits of home-cooked meals without the stress and time commitment traditionally associated with cooking.

While the integration of robots in the kitchen offers numerous advantages, it also raises important questions about the future of food and dining. As technology continues to advance, it is crucial to consider the impact on culinary traditions, job opportunities for chefs, and the overall dining experience. By thoughtfully integrating robotics into the culinary world, we can harness the potential of these innovations to enhance our lives while preserving the rich cultural heritage that makes food such a powerful force for connection.

4

Chapter 4: The Social Impact of Automated Dining

The rise of automated dining, characterized by the use of robots and artificial intelligence in food preparation and service, has the potential to transform the social dynamics of eating. On one hand, automation can enhance convenience and accessibility, making it easier for people to access high-quality meals regardless of their location or lifestyle. For instance, automated food delivery services and smart vending machines can provide nutritious and affordable meals to underserved communities, reducing food insecurity and promoting public health.

Moreover, automated dining can create new opportunities for social interaction and engagement. Virtual dining experiences, facilitated by augmented reality and telepresence technologies, allow people to share meals and conversations with loved ones across the globe. These innovations can help bridge the gap between physical distance and social connection, fostering a sense of togetherness and community in an increasingly digital world. Additionally, the rise of food tech startups and innovation hubs can create new spaces for collaboration and creativity, bringing together chefs, engineers, and entrepreneurs to explore the future of food.

However, the widespread adoption of automated dining also raises important ethical and societal considerations. The displacement of traditional food service jobs by robots and AI could have significant economic implications, particularly for low-income and marginalized communities. It is essential to ensure that the benefits of automation are distributed equitably and that workers are provided with opportunities for retraining and upskilling. Furthermore, the reliance on technology in food production and distribution raises questions about data privacy, security, and the potential for algorithmic bias in decision-making processes.

To navigate these challenges, it is crucial to adopt a holistic and inclusive approach to automated dining. By engaging diverse stakeholders, including policymakers, industry leaders, and community representatives, we can develop strategies that promote the responsible and ethical integration of technology in the culinary world. In doing so, we can harness the potential of automated dining to enhance our lives while ensuring that the social fabric of food remains intact.

5

Chapter 5: The Intersection of Tradition and Innovation

The culinary world is a dynamic landscape where tradition and innovation intersect, creating a rich tapestry of flavors, techniques, and experiences. This interplay between the old and the new is evident in the way chefs and home cooks alike draw inspiration from diverse culinary traditions while embracing cutting-edge technologies and modern trends. By blending time-honored practices with innovative approaches, we can create unique and memorable dining experiences that celebrate the best of both worlds.

One of the most exciting aspects of this intersection is the fusion of culinary cultures. Chefs around the globe are increasingly experimenting with cross-cultural cuisines, combining ingredients and techniques from different culinary traditions to create novel and exciting dishes. This culinary fusion not only expands our palates but also fosters a deeper appreciation for the diversity and interconnectedness of the world's food cultures. As a result, diners can embark on a gastronomic journey that transcends geographical and cultural boundaries.

Innovation in the culinary world is not limited to the kitchen; it also extends to the way we grow, source, and consume food. Sustainable farming practices, such as vertical farming and aquaponics, are revolutionizing agriculture by reducing environmental impact and promoting food security. Additionally, the rise of plant-based and alternative protein products reflects a growing awareness of the need for more sustainable and ethical food choices. These innovations are transforming the way we think about food, encouraging us to consider the broader implications of our dietary habits on the planet and future generations.

As we embrace culinary innovation, it is essential to preserve the rich heritage of traditional food practices. By celebrating and honoring the culinary wisdom passed down through generations, we can ensure that these traditions continue to thrive in the modern world. This balance between tradition and innovation allows us to create a culinary landscape that is both rooted in history and forward-looking, offering endless possibilities for creativity, connection, and enjoyment.

6

Chapter 6: Dining in the Digital Age

The digital age has ushered in a new era of dining, characterized by the seamless integration of technology into our culinary experiences. From online recipe platforms and food blogs to virtual cooking classes and social media food influencers, the way we discover, share, and enjoy food has been transformed by the digital revolution. These digital innovations have democratized access to culinary knowledge, empowering individuals to explore new cuisines, improve their cooking skills, and connect with like-minded food enthusiasts.

One of the most significant impacts of the digital age on dining is the rise of online food communities. These virtual spaces provide a platform for people to share their culinary creations, exchange tips and recipes, and engage in discussions about food and cooking. Online food communities foster a sense of belonging and camaraderie, allowing individuals to connect with others who share their passion for food. Through these interactions, people can learn from each other's experiences, gain inspiration, through their culinary journeys, and develop a deeper appreciation for the diverse world of food.

The digital age has also given rise to a new wave of food influencers who share their culinary expertise and creativity with a global audience. These influencers, often chefs, home cooks, or food enthusiasts, use social media platforms to showcase their recipes, cooking techniques, and dining experiences. By providing a glimpse into their culinary worlds, they inspire others to experiment in the kitchen and explore new flavors and cuisines. The influence of these digital tastemakers has reshaped the way we approach food, encouraging innovation and creativity in the kitchen.

Virtual cooking classes and online culinary workshops have further revolutionized the way we learn about food. These digital platforms provide accessible and interactive opportunities for individuals to improve their cooking skills and gain insights from expert chefs and culinary professionals. Whether it's a live-streamed cooking demonstration or an on-demand tutorial, these virtual learning experiences make it easier than ever to master new techniques and expand our culinary repertoire.

As we navigate the digital age, it is essential to recognize the value of both online and offline culinary experiences. While digital platforms offer convenience and connectivity, the tactile and sensory aspects of cooking and dining in the physical world remain irreplaceable. By embracing the best of both worlds, we can create a harmonious blend of digital innovation and traditional culinary practices, enriching our lives and fostering a deeper connection to the food we eat.

7

Chapter 7: The Role of Technology in Sustainable Food Practices

Technology has the potential to play a significant role in promoting sustainable food practices and addressing some of the most pressing challenges facing our global food system. From precision agriculture and vertical farming to lab-grown meat and food waste reduction technologies, innovative solutions are emerging that can help create a more resilient and sustainable food future.

Precision agriculture, which involves the use of data and technology to optimize crop production, is revolutionizing the way we grow food. By leveraging tools such as sensors, drones, and satellite imagery, farmers can monitor soil health, track crop growth, and make data-driven decisions about irrigation, fertilization, and pest management. This approach not only increases crop yields but also reduces the environmental impact of farming by minimizing the use of water, chemicals, and other resources.

Vertical farming is another promising innovation that is transforming the way we produce food. By growing crops in vertically stacked layers within controlled environments, vertical farms can maximize land use efficiency and reduce the need for pesticides and herbicides. These farms can be established in urban areas, bringing food production closer to consumers and reducing the carbon footprint associated with transportation. Additionally, vertical farming allows for year-round cultivation, ensuring a consistent supply of fresh produce regardless of seasonal variations.

Lab-grown meat, also known as cultured meat, represents a groundbreaking development in the quest for more sustainable and ethical food production. By cultivating animal cells in a lab setting, researchers can produce meat without the need for traditional livestock farming, which is a significant contributor to greenhouse gas emissions and deforestation. While lab-grown meat is still in its early stages, it has the potential to provide a viable alternative to conventional meat production, offering a more environmentally friendly and humane option for consumers.

Technology is also playing a crucial role in addressing food waste, which is a major global issue. Innovative solutions such as food tracking apps, smart packaging, and automated inventory management systems can help reduce food waste by improving supply chain efficiency and enabling consumers to better manage their food purchases and consumption. By harnessing the power of technology, we can create a more sustainable and equitable food system that benefits both people and the planet.

8

Chapter 8: The Future of Dining: Trends and Innovations

The future of dining is shaped by a variety of trends and innovations that are redefining the way we think about food and dining experiences. One of the most notable trends is the increasing focus on sustainability and ethical consumption. As consumers become more conscious of the environmental and social impact of their food choices, there is a growing demand for sustainable and ethically sourced ingredients. This shift is driving the development of plant-based and alternative protein products, as well as the adoption of sustainable farming and fishing practices.

Another significant trend is the rise of experiential dining, which emphasizes immersive and interactive dining experiences. Restaurants and food establishments are increasingly incorporating elements of storytelling, theatrics, and multisensory engagement into their offerings, creating memorable and unique experiences for diners. From themed dining events to interactive cooking classes, experiential dining is transforming the way we connect with food and each other.

Technology continues to play a pivotal role in shaping the future of dining. The integration of artificial intelligence, robotics, and automation in food preparation and service is paving the way for new dining experiences that prioritize efficiency, precision, and personalization. For example, AI-powered recommendation systems can tailor menu suggestions to individual preferences, while robotic chefs can prepare complex dishes with consistency and speed. These technological advancements are enhancing the dining experience by offering greater convenience and customization.

The future of dining also includes the growing popularity of food delivery and meal kit services. These services provide consumers with convenient and flexible options for enjoying restaurant-quality meals at home. With the rise of ghost kitchens and virtual restaurants, the food delivery landscape is becoming more diverse and competitive, offering a wide range of culinary options to suit different tastes and preferences. As these trends and innovations continue to evolve, the future of dining promises to be dynamic, diverse, and deeply connected to the values and aspirations of the modern consumer.

9

Chapter 9: The Impact of Globalization on Food Culture

G lobalization has had a profound impact on food culture, leading to the exchange of culinary traditions, ingredients, and techniques across borders. This interconnectedness has resulted in the fusion of diverse food cultures, creating a rich and diverse culinary landscape that reflects the complexity and dynamism of our global society. As people travel, migrate, and interact with different cultures, they bring their culinary heritage with them, enriching the food culture of their new communities.

One of the most visible effects of globalization on food culture is the proliferation of international cuisines. In major cities around the world, it is now possible to find restaurants and food establishments that offer a wide range of global dishes, from sushi and tacos to curry and kebabs. This culinary diversity not only expands our palates but also fosters cross-cultural understanding and appreciation. By exploring and enjoying different cuisines, we can gain insights into the history, values, and traditions of other cultures.

Globalization has also facilitated the exchange of culinary knowledge and techniques. Chefs and food enthusiasts can now access a wealth of information and resources online, allowing them to learn about and experiment with different cooking methods and ingredients. This exchange of knowledge has led to the emergence of innovative fusion dishes that combine elements from multiple culinary traditions, creating new and exciting flavors. Additionally, the global food supply chain has made it possible to source exotic ingredients from around the world, further expanding the possibilities for culinary creativity.

While globalization has brought many benefits to food culture, it also presents challenges. The widespread availability of fast food and processed foods has contributed to changes in dietary habits and the rise of health issues such as obesity and diabetes. Moreover, the global demand for certain ingredients has led to environmental degradation and the exploitation of natural resources. To address these challenges, it is important to promote sustainable and ethical food practices that respect both cultural heritage and the environment. By doing so, we can ensure that the impact of globalization on food culture is positive and inclusive, fostering a deeper connection to the world's culinary diversity.

10

Chapter 10: Food and Community: Building Connections Through Meals

Food has always been a powerful tool for building community and fostering connections. Whether it's a family gathering, a neighborhood potluck, or a cultural festival, shared meals create opportunities for people to come together, share their stories, and strengthen social bonds. In a world where people are increasingly isolated and disconnected, food can serve as a unifying force that brings individuals and communities closer.

One of the most effective ways to build community through food is by organizing communal dining experiences. These events, which can range from intimate dinner parties to large-scale community feasts, provide a platform for people to connect over a shared love of food. By breaking bread together, individuals can engage in meaningful conversations, exchange ideas, and build lasting relationships. Communal dining experiences also promote inclusivity by bringing together people from diverse backgrounds and fostering a sense of belonging.

Cultural and religious festivals centered around food are another important aspect of building community. These events celebrate the culinary traditions and heritage of different cultures, providing an opportunity for people to learn about and appreciate the diversity of the world's food cultures. From

Diwali and Thanksgiving to Lunar New Year and Eid al-Fitr, these festivals highlight the role of food in bringing people together and creating a sense of shared identity.

Food-based initiatives and organizations also play a crucial role in building community. Community gardens, food co-ops, and farmers' markets are just a few examples of how food can be used to create spaces for social interaction and cooperation. These initiatives not only promote access to fresh and healthy food but also provide opportunities for individuals to collaborate, share resources, and support each other. By fostering a sense of community and cooperation, food-based initiatives can help address social issues such as food insecurity, isolation, and inequality.

11

Chapter 11: The Ethics of Eating: Navigating Food Choices

The ethics of eating is a complex and multifaceted topic that encompasses a wide range of considerations, from animal welfare and environmental sustainability to social justice and cultural sensitivity. As consumers become more aware of the ethical implications of their food choices, there is a growing demand for transparency and accountability in the food industry. Navigating these ethical considerations requires a thoughtful and informed approach to food consumption.

One of the primary ethical concerns in the food industry is animal welfare. The treatment of animals in factory farming and industrial agriculture has raised significant ethical questions about the humane treatment of livestock. Consumers who prioritize animal welfare may choose to support practices such as free-range farming, organic production, and plant-based diets. By making conscious choices about the sources of their food, individuals can contribute to the promotion of more humane and ethical food production practices.

Environmental sustainability is another critical aspect of ethical eating. The production, transportation, and disposal of food have significant environmental impacts, including greenhouse gas emissions, deforestation, and water pollution. Ethical eaters may choose to support sustainable farming practices, such as organic agriculture, regenerative farming, and locally sourced produce. By making environmentally conscious food choices, individuals can reduce their ecological footprint and contribute to the preservation of natural resources for future generations.

Social justice is another important consideration in the ethics of eating. The food industry is often marked by issues such as labor exploitation, unequal access to nutritious food, and food deserts in marginalized communities. Consumers who prioritize social justice may choose to support fair trade products, community-supported agriculture (CSA), and initiatives that promote food equity and accessibility. By advocating for fair labor practices and supporting local food systems, individuals can help create a more just and equitable food landscape.

Cultural sensitivity and respect for culinary traditions are also essential components of ethical eating. In our increasingly globalized world, it is important to approach diverse food cultures with an open mind and a willingness to learn. This means avoiding cultural appropriation, respecting the origins and significance of traditional dishes, and supporting authentic representations of different cuisines. By celebrating and honoring the culinary heritage of various cultures, we can foster a deeper appreciation for the diversity and richness of the world's food traditions.

12

Chapter 12: A Vision for the Future: Food, Robots, and Society

As we look to the future, the convergence of food, robots, and society holds exciting possibilities for creating a more connected and harmonious world. The advancements in technology and automation have the potential to transform the way we grow, prepare, and consume food, making it more sustainable, efficient, and enjoyable. At the same time, it is essential to preserve the cultural and social significance of food, ensuring that it remains a powerful force for connection and community.

One of the key aspects of this vision for the future is the integration of technology in a way that enhances, rather than replaces, human creativity and ingenuity. By leveraging the precision and efficiency of robots and artificial intelligence, we can free up human chefs and food enthusiasts to focus on innovation, experimentation, and the art of cooking. This collaboration between humans and machines can lead to new culinary discoveries and a deeper appreciation for the craft of food preparation.

Another important element of this vision is the promotion of sustainability and ethical practices in the food industry. By embracing sustainable farming methods, reducing food waste, and supporting fair labor practices, we can create a food system that is not only efficient but also equitable and environmentally responsible. Technological advancements, such as precision agriculture and lab-grown meat, can play a crucial role in achieving these goals, providing innovative solutions to the challenges facing our global food system.

Finally, the future of food should prioritize the social and cultural aspects of dining, fostering a sense of community and connection. Whether it's through communal dining experiences, cultural festivals, or virtual dining platforms, food has the power to bring people together and create shared moments of joy and celebration. By honoring the traditions and heritage of different food cultures, we can ensure that the future of dining is inclusive, diverse, and deeply rooted in our shared humanity.

In conclusion, the intersection of food, robots, and society presents a unique opportunity to create a more connected and harmonious world. By embracing technological advancements, promoting sustainability, and celebrating the cultural significance of food, we can build a future where food continues to bring us together and enrich our lives in meaningful ways.

13

Chapter 13: The Emotional Connection: Food and Memory

Food has a profound ability to evoke memories and emotions, creating a powerful connection between our past and present. The taste, smell, and texture of certain dishes can transport us back to significant moments in our lives, bringing forth memories of loved ones, special occasions, and cultural traditions. This emotional connection to food is deeply ingrained in our experiences and plays a crucial role in shaping our identities and sense of belonging.

For many, family recipes passed down through generations hold a special place in their hearts. These dishes are not just a source of nourishment but also a way to honor and preserve the culinary heritage of our ancestors. The act of preparing and sharing these recipes can evoke feelings of nostalgia, comfort, and pride, reinforcing the bonds between family members and connecting us to our cultural roots. Food, in this sense, becomes a vessel for storytelling, allowing us to share our histories and traditions with future generations.

The emotional connection to food also extends to communal dining experiences. Sharing a meal with others can create lasting memories and foster a sense of community and togetherness. Whether it's a holiday feast, a celebratory dinner, or a casual gathering with friends, the act of eating together strengthens social bonds and creates a sense of belonging. These shared experiences become cherished memories that we carry with us throughout our lives.

In the digital age, the emotional connection to food is further amplified by social media and online food communities. People share their culinary creations, food stories, and dining experiences with a global audience, creating a virtual archive of memories and emotions. This digital exchange of food memories helps us connect with others, celebrate our shared love of food, and preserve the culinary moments that shape our lives.

14

Chapter 14: The Science of Flavor: Understanding Taste and Aroma

The science of flavor is a fascinating field that explores the complex interplay between taste, aroma, and our sensory perceptions. Flavor is not just a simple combination of taste and smell; it is a multidimensional experience that involves a range of sensory inputs, including texture, temperature, and even the sound of food. Understanding the science behind flavor can enhance our appreciation of food and elevate our culinary experiences.

Taste, one of the primary components of flavor, is detected by taste buds on our tongue. There are five basic tastes: sweet, salty, sour, bitter, and umami. Each taste receptor responds to specific molecules in food, sending signals to the brain that create the perception of flavor. For example, the sweetness of sugar is detected by receptors that respond to glucose, while the umami taste of soy sauce is detected by receptors that respond to glutamate.

Aroma, another crucial component of flavor, is detected by olfactory receptors in the nose. When we eat, the aromas of food are released and travel to the olfactory receptors, creating a complex and nuanced perception of flavor. The sense of smell is highly sensitive and can detect thousands of different odor molecules, contributing to the rich and diverse world of food aromas. The combination of taste and aroma creates the unique flavor profile of each dish, making it an unforgettable experience.

In addition to taste and aroma, other sensory factors such as texture and temperature play a significant role in our perception of flavor. The crunch of a fresh vegetable, the creaminess of a dessert, or the warmth of a hot soup can enhance the overall dining experience and influence our enjoyment of food. The science of flavor also takes into account individual differences in taste perception, which can be influenced by genetics, cultural background, and personal preferences.

By exploring the science of flavor, chefs and home cooks can create more harmonious and balanced dishes that appeal to our senses. This knowledge allows us to experiment with different flavor combinations, techniques, and ingredients, expanding our culinary horizons and deepening our appreciation for the art of cooking.

15

Chapter 15: Food and Health: Nourishing Body and Mind

Food is not only a source of pleasure and connection but also a fundamental pillar of our health and well-being. The nutrients we obtain from food play a crucial role in supporting our physical and mental health, influencing everything from energy levels and immune function to mood and cognitive performance. Understanding the relationship between food and health can empower us to make informed choices that nourish both our body and mind.

A balanced and diverse diet is essential for providing the nutrients our bodies need to function optimally. Macronutrients such as carbohydrates, proteins, and fats provide the energy necessary for daily activities, while micronutrients such as vitamins and minerals support various physiological processes. For example, vitamin C is vital for immune function, calcium is crucial for bone health, and omega-3 fatty acids are important for brain function. By consuming a variety of nutrient-rich foods, we can ensure that our bodies receive the essential components needed for overall health.

In addition to physical health, food also plays a significant role in mental well-being. Certain nutrients, such as omega-3 fatty acids, B vitamins, and antioxidants, have been shown to support brain health and cognitive function. Moreover, the act of eating itself can have a positive impact on mental health.

Sharing a meal with others, practicing mindful eating, and enjoying the sensory pleasures of food can promote relaxation, reduce stress, and enhance mood.

The relationship between food and health extends beyond individual well-being to encompass broader societal and environmental considerations. Sustainable and ethical food practices, such as supporting local farmers, reducing food waste, and choosing plant-based options, contribute to the health of our communities and the planet. By making conscious food choices, we can create a positive impact on our own health and the well-being of future generations.

As we navigate the complexities of food and health, it is important to adopt a holistic and balanced approach. By prioritizing nutrient-dense foods, fostering positive eating habits, and considering the broader implications of our food choices, we can nourish our bodies and minds while contributing to a healthier and more sustainable world.

16

Chapter 16: Culinary Creativity: The Art of Innovation in the Kitchen

Culinary creativity is the driving force behind the evolution of food and dining experiences. It is the ability to experiment, innovate, and push the boundaries of traditional cooking to create new and exciting dishes. The art of culinary creativity involves not only technical skills and knowledge but also imagination, curiosity, and a passion for exploring the unknown. By embracing creativity in the kitchen, chefs and home cooks alike can elevate their culinary endeavors and delight the senses of diners.

One of the key aspects of culinary creativity is the willingness to experiment with different ingredients, flavors, and techniques. This may involve combining unexpected elements to create harmonious and surprising flavor profiles, or reinterpreting classic dishes with a modern twist. For example, molecular gastronomy, a culinary movement that incorporates scientific principles and techniques, has given rise to innovative creations such as foams, gels, and edible spheres. These avant-garde dishes challenge our perceptions of food and open up new possibilities for culinary expression.

Creativity in the kitchen is not limited to professional chefs; home cooks can also embrace innovative approaches to elevate their everyday meals. Whether it's trying out a new recipe, experimenting with fusion cuisine, or incorporating seasonal ingredients, culinary creativity allows individuals to infuse their cooking with personality and flair. The process of creating and sharing these unique dishes can be a source of joy, satisfaction, and connection with others.

In addition to flavor and technique, presentation is an important aspect of culinary creativity. The visual appeal of a dish can enhance the overall dining experience and make it more memorable. Chefs and home cooks can experiment with plating techniques, color combinations, and garnishes to create visually stunning presentations that captivate the eyes and stimulate the appetite. The art of plating transforms food into an edible masterpiece, showcasing the creativity and craftsmanship behind each dish.

Ultimately, culinary creativity is about pushing the boundaries of what is possible in the kitchen and celebrating the endless possibilities of food. By embracing innovation, curiosity, and a spirit of adventure, we can create culinary experiences that inspire, delight, and connect us to the rich and diverse world of food.

17

Chapter 17: Food as Cultural Diplomacy: Bridging Divides

Food has the unique ability to serve as a form of cultural diplomacy, fostering understanding and cooperation between nations and communities. By sharing and celebrating diverse culinary traditions, food can bridge cultural divides and promote peaceful interactions in a way that transcends language and political barriers. The act of breaking bread together creates opportunities for dialogue, mutual respect, and collaboration, making food a powerful tool for cultural exchange and diplomacy.

Culinary diplomacy initiatives, also known as gastro-diplomacy, have gained recognition as effective means of fostering international relations. Governments, cultural organizations, and chefs often engage in culinary exchanges, food festivals, and culinary tours to showcase their country's cuisine and promote cross-cultural understanding. These initiatives provide a platform for people from different backgrounds to come together, share their culinary heritage, and build positive relationships based on shared experiences and mutual appreciation.

One notable example of culinary diplomacy is the use of food in diplomatic events and state dinners. These occasions often feature dishes that highlight the host country's culinary traditions while also incorporating elements from the guest country's cuisine. By doing so, state dinners create a sense of hospitality and respect, fostering goodwill and strengthening diplomatic ties. The inclusion of food in diplomatic settings underscores its role as a universal language that can convey messages of friendship, cooperation, and cultural pride.

Culinary diplomacy is not limited to formal events; it can also take place at the grassroots level. Food festivals, cultural exchange programs, and community-based culinary initiatives provide opportunities for people to engage in cross-cultural interactions and learn about each other's culinary traditions. These grassroots efforts contribute to building cultural bridges and fostering a sense of global community. By celebrating the diversity of food cultures and embracing culinary diplomacy, we can create a more connected and harmonious world, where food serves as a catalyst for understanding, collaboration, and peace.

The Connected Table: How Food, Robots, and Society Bring Us Together

In "The Connected Table," you'll embark on a captivating journey through the evolving world of food, technology, and community. This book delves into the universal language of food and how it brings people together across cultural divides. From the evolution of dining practices to the cutting-edge innovations of robotic chefs, you'll explore how technology is revolutionizing the culinary landscape.

Each chapter takes you deeper into the intersection of tradition and innovation, revealing how ancient culinary practices coexist with modern advancements. You'll discover the impact of automated dining on society, the emotional connection between food and memory, and the science behind taste and aroma. The book also addresses the ethical considerations of our food choices, the role of technology in promoting sustainability, and the power of food as a tool for cultural diplomacy.

With engaging narratives and thought-provoking insights, "The Connected Table" celebrates the rich tapestry of flavors, traditions, and experiences that food offers. It envisions a future where food, robots, and society come together to create a more connected, sustainable, and harmonious world. Whether you're a food enthusiast, a tech aficionado, or someone curious

CHAPTER 17: FOOD AS CULTURAL DIPLOMACY: BRIDGING DIVIDES

about the future of dining, this book offers a compelling exploration of how food and technology can unite us in our shared humanity.

www.ingramcontent.com/pod-product-compliance
Lightning Source LLC
LaVergne TN
LVHW020458080526
838202LV00057B/6029